# First World War
## and Army of Occupation
# War Diary
## France, Belgium and Germany

60 DIVISION
Headquarters, Branches and Services
Adjutant and Quarter-Master General
31 May 1916 - 30 November 1916

WO95/3026/5

The Naval & Military Press Ltd
www.nmarchive.com
Published in association with The National Archives

Published by

## The Naval & Military Press Ltd

Unit 10 Ridgewood Industrial Park,

Uckfield, East Sussex,

TN22 5QE England

Tel: +44 (0) 1825 749494

www.naval-military-press.com

www.nmarchive.com

*This diary has been reprinted in facsimile from the original. Any imperfections are inevitably reproduced and the quality may fall short of modern type and cartographic standards.*

© **Crown Copyright**
**Images reproduced by permission of The National Archives, London, England, 2015.**

# Contents

| Document type | Place/Title | Date From | Date To |
|---|---|---|---|
| Heading | WO95/3026/5 | | |
| Heading | Intelligence Summary 60th (London) Division HQ Inf 60D Vol I | | |
| War Diary | Sutton Veny Camp | 31/05/1916 | 16/06/1916 |
| War Diary | Sutton Veny | 18/06/1916 | 30/06/1916 |
| War Diary | Sutton Veny | 31/05/1916 | 30/06/1916 |
| Heading | War Diary A.Q. Branch H.Q. 60th (London) Divn June 1916 (From May 31 1916 To June 30th 1916) | | |
| War Diary | Sutton Veny | 31/05/1916 | 30/06/1916 |
| War Diary | Villers Chatel | 01/07/1916 | 13/07/1916 |
| War Diary | Hermaville | 14/07/1916 | 31/07/1916 |
| Heading | War Diary A & Q Branch H.Q. 60th (London) Divn From August 1st 1916 To August 31st 1916 | | |
| War Diary | Hermaville | 01/08/1916 | 30/09/1916 |
| Heading | War Diary A.Q. Branch 60th Division From 1st Oct 1916 To 31st Oct 1916 Vol 5 | | |
| War Diary | Hermaville | 01/10/1916 | 26/10/1916 |
| War Diary | Houvin | 27/10/1916 | 27/10/1916 |
| War Diary | Frohen Le Grande | 28/10/1916 | 28/10/1916 |
| War Diary | Bernaville | 29/10/1916 | 02/11/1916 |
| War Diary | Ailly Le Haut Clocher | 03/11/1916 | 24/11/1916 |
| War Diary | In Train | 25/11/1916 | 29/11/1916 |
| War Diary | At Sea | 30/11/1916 | 30/11/1916 |

WO 95/30266

HD Int 60D

Intelligence Summary.
—–—
60th (London) Division.

Original

60 London Division
WAR DIARY
—of—
INTELLIGENCE SUMMARY.
(Erase heading not required.)

Army Form C. 2118.

Instructions regarding War Diaries and Intelligence Summaries are contained in F.S. Regs., Part II. and the Staff Manual respectively. Title pages will be prepared in manuscript.

| Hour, Date, Place | Summary of Events and Information | Remarks and references to Appendices |
|---|---|---|
| 1916 | | |
| 31 May Sutton Veny Camp. | H.M. arrived Heytesbury 11 am – Review Troops of 60 London Division 11.15 a.m. – Received Presentations of Officers after Review – left Warminster R.S. Station 1.30 p.m. | |
| 31 May Sutton Veny Camp | Under instruction from Southern Command Head Quarters commenced 15 June to all ranks 4 days leave as provided by Army Council Instruction No. 1041 of 1916. | |
| 12 June Sutton Veny Camp | Except for men of drafts who could not avail themselves of leave until they had been through G.M.C. – all Officers & men returned from 4 days leave. | |
| 14 June " " | War Office Q.M.G. 2/1006 d/13 June 1916 received from Southern Command d/13 June 1916 | |
| 15 June " " | Orders for Entrainment – Detraining – for Supplies & Transport issued to all Units under 60 London Division No Q 540 Capt. HUME GORE G.S.O. 3 and 13 Officers to Landing & Entraining Duties leave WARMINSTER for SOUTHAMPTON and HAVRE | |
| 16 June " " | War Office Time Table Received d/16.6.16 Cancelled 17.6.16 | |

Forms/C. 2118/10

**60th London Division**

**WAR DIARY** or **INTELLIGENCE SUMMARY** (Continued)

Army Form C. 2118.

1916

| Place | Date | Hour | Summary of Events and Information | Remarks and references to Appendices |
|---|---|---|---|---|
| SUTTON VENY | JUNE 18 | | Major McCall QMG Major McCall and 5 Officers including DADOS with 5 Motor Cars proceed to FOLKESTONE for BOULOGNE | (Sgd) |
| " | 19 | | CRS C 106044 of 18 June 1916 regarding DAC stores which should be sent in Vans in lieu of the 74 wagons returned. | (Sgd) |
| " | 22 | 3.30 pm | Divisional Hd Qrs entrained Warminster Railway Station — Arrived SOUTHAMPTON Docks 5.55 pm — S.S PANCRAS left docks at 8 pm | (Sgd) |
| " | 23 | 9 am | Arrived HAVRE. 2/15 LR & 10 Monts en Ternois — 2/14 LR — BUNEVILLE | (Sgd) |
| | 24 | 4 pm | Div. Hd Qrs Left HAVRE — 2/13 LR — PENIN 2/14 AVERDOINGT — 2/15 MONTS EN TERNOIS | (Sgd) — PIONEERS at TERNAS |
| | 25 | 12.15 | Arrived ST POL and proceeded to FLERS — CHATEAU DE FLERS 2/13 — ECOIVRES. 2/14 MAROEUIL 2/15 PENIN 2/16 ABER DOINGT — 2/17 ECOIVRES (FLERS) | (Sgd) PIONEERS at TERNAS |
| | 26 | | + 2/13 MONT ST ELOI 2/14 MAROEUIL 2/15 MAROEUIL 2/16 ECROIVES — 2/17 PENIN (at LOUEZ/ACQ) 2/18 ABERDOINGT — 2/19 CROISETTE 2/20 BLANGERMONT — 3/3 + 2/4 to LOUEZ & MAROUIL (2/3 + 2/4→) 2/15 ACQ & MT S'ELOI — Remainder 180 Brigade | (Sgd) |
| | 27 | | HQ 179 Brigade from PENIN to ECROIVRES — 2/17 ACQ — 2/16 TS ACQ + MT S'ELOI — 300 RFA Brigade + PENIN — 181 TC CHELERS from Railway Station ST POL + PETIT HOUVAIN — CAPELLE FERMONT + LAESSET and ACQ and 303 RFA to ACQ & CAPELLE FERMONT | (Sgd) |
| | 28 | 8 am | Div. HQ + VILLERS CHATEL 1/6 Fd Company to MT S'ELOI — HAUTE ASCOT + HAUTE AVESNES 2/21 + 2/22 1Bgdes LOUEZ + MAROUIL ST MICHEL SUR TERNOIS | (Sgd) |
| | 29 | | DAC arrived ST POL proceeded St MICHEL SUR TERNOIS | (Sgd) |
| | 30 | | 2 Companies 2/19 to BOIS DE BRAY & BOIS DE ALLEUX | (Sgd) |

P. Blake S—
A A & QMG
60 London Div
1 July 1916

Duplicate

60th London Division
WAR DIARY
—
INTELLIGENCE SUMMARY.
(Erase heading not required.)

Army Form C. 2118.

Instructions regarding War Diaries and Intelligence Summaries are contained in F. S. Regs., Part II. and the Staff Manual respectively. Title pages will be prepared in manuscript.

| Place | Date | Hour | Summary of Events and Information | Remarks and references to Appendices |
|---|---|---|---|---|
| 1916 SUTTON VENY | May 31 | | HIS MAJESTY arrived HEYTESBURY 11 a.m. Review troops of 60th (London) Division, 11.15 a.m. Received Presentations of Officers after Review - Left WARMINSTER Railway Station 1.30 pm. | |
| " | 31 | | Under instructions from Southern Command Headquarters commenced to give to all ranks 4 days leave as provided by Army Council Instruction No. 1041 of 1916. | |
| " | June 12 | | Except for men of drafts who could not avail themselves of leave until they had been through G.M.C. - all officers and men returned from 4 days leave. | |
| " | 14 | | War Office Q.M.G. 2/1006 d/ 13th June, 1916, received from Southern Command d/ 13th June, 1916. | |
| " | 15 | | Orders for Entraining, Detraining, and for Supplies and Transport issued to all Units under 60th (London) Division No. Q 540. | |
| " | 15 | | Capt. HUME GORE, G.S.O. 3, and 13 Officers for Landing and Entraining Duties leave WARMINSTER for SOUTHAMPTON and HAVRE. | |
| " | 16 | | War Office Time Table received d/ 16th June, 1916 - Circulated 17th June, 1916. | |

P.T.O.

Army Form C. 2118.

60th London Division

# WAR DIARY
## INTELLIGENCE SUMMARY.
*(Erase heading not required.)*

(Contined)

Instructions regarding War Diaries and Intelligence Summaries are contained in F. S. Regs., Part II. and the Staff Manual respectively. Title pages will be prepared in manuscript.

| Place | Date | Hour | Summary of Events and Information | Remarks and references to Appendices |
|---|---|---|---|---|
| 1916. SUTTON VENY | June 18 | | MAJOR McCALL and 5 Officers including D.A.D.O.S. with 5 Motor Cars proceed to FOLKESTONE for BOULOGNE. | |
| " | 19 | | C.R.S.C. 106044 (O) d/ 18th June, 1916, regarding D.A.C. Stores which should be sent in Vans in place of the 74 wagons returned. | |
| " | 22 | 3.30 p.m. | Divisional Headquarters entrained WARMINSTER Railway Station – Arrived SOUTHAMPTON DOCKS 5.55 p.m. S.S. PANCRAS left Docks at 8 p.m. | |
| | 23 | 8 a.m. | Arrived Havre. 2/13th Lon. Regt. to MONTS EN TERNOIS – 2/14th Lond. Regt. to BUNEVILLE. | |
| | 24 | 4 p.m. | Divl. Headquarters left HAVRE – 2/13th Lon. Regt. – PENIN – 2/14th – AVERDOINGT – 2/15th MONTS EN TERNOIS – Pioneers – TERNAS | |
| | 25 | 12.15 | Arrived ST. POL and proceeded to FLERS – CHATEAU DE FLERS. 2/13th Battn – ECOIVRES, 2/14th Battn. – MAROEUIL, 2/15th – PENIN, 2/16th ABERDOINGT, 2/17th ECOIVRES (FLERS), Pioneers from TERNAS to LOUEZ & ACQ. | |
| | 26 | | 2/13th, MONT ST ELOI, 2/14th MAROEUIL, 2/15th MAROEUIL, 2/16th ECOIVRES, 2/17th PENIN, 2/18th ABERDOINGT, 2/19th CROISETTE, 2/20th BLANGERMONT, 3/3rd R.E. & 2/4th to LOUEZ & MAROEUIL ¶1/3 on 25th | |
| | 27 | | H.Q. 179th Bde. from PENIN to ECOIVRES, 2/17th to ACQ, 2/18th to ACQ & MONT ST ELOI, Remainder 180th Bde. to PENIN, 181st to CHELERS from Railway Station ST. POL & PETIT HOUVAIN, 300th R.F.A. Bde. to LAESSET and ACQ and 303rd R.F.A. to ACQ & CAPELLE FERMONT. | |
| | 28 | 8 a.m. | Divl. Hd.Qrs. to VILLERS CHATEL, 1/6th Fld. Coy. to MONT ST ELOI, Hd.Qrs.Coy. A.S.C. to HAUTE AVESNES, 2/21st & 2/22nd Battns. to LOUEZ and MAROEUIL. | |
| | 29 | | D.A.C. arrived ST. POL proceeded ST MICHEL SURTERNOIS. | |
| | 30 | | 2 Companies 2/19th to BOIS DE BRAY & BOIS DE ALLEUX. | |

[Signed]
A.A. & Q.M.G. Division
60th L. Division

1 July 1916

Secret.

Vol 1

War Diary

A. Q Branch, H.Q. 60th (London) Divn

June 1916.
(From May 31 1916 to June 30th 1916)

Army Form C. 2118.

# WAR DIARY

## INTELLIGENCE SUMMARY.

(Erase heading not required.)

Instructions regarding War Diaries and Intelligence Summaries are contained in F. S. Regs., Part II. and the Staff Manual respectively. Title pages will be prepared in manuscript.

| Place | Date | Hour | Summary of Events and Information | Remarks and references to Appendices |
|---|---|---|---|---|
| 1916 SUTTON VENY | May 31 | | HIS MAJESTY arrived HEYTESBURY 11 a.m. Review troops of 60th (London) Division, 11.15 a.m. Received Presentations of Officers after Review - Left WARMINSTER Railway Station 1.30 pm. | |
| " | 31 | | Under instructions from Southern Command Headquarters commenced to give to all ranks 4 days leave as provided by Army Council Instruction No. 1041 of 1916. | |
| " | June 12 | | Except for men of drafts who could not avail themselves of leave until they had been through G.M.C. - all officers and men returned from 4 days leave. | |
| " | 14 | | War Office Q.M.G. 2/1006 d/ 13th June, 1916, received from Southern Command d/ 13th June, 1916. | |
| " | 15 | | Orders for Entraining, Detraining, and for Supplies and Transport issued to all Units under 60th (London) Division No. Q 540. | |
| " | 15 | | Capt. HUME GORE, G.S.O. 3, and 15 Officers for Landing and Entraining Duties leave WARMINSTER for SOUTHAMPTON and HAVRE. | |
| " | 16 | | War Office Time Table received d/ 16th June, 1916 - Circulated 17th June, 1916. | |

Army Form C. 2118.

# WAR DIARY
## or
## INTELLIGENCE SUMMARY.
*(Erase heading not required.)*

Instructions regarding War Diaries and Intelligence Summaries are contained in F.S. Regs., Part II. and the Staff Manual respectively. Title pages will be prepared in manuscript.

| Place | Date | Hour | Summary of Events and Information | Remarks and references to Appendices |
|---|---|---|---|---|
| 1916. SUTTON VENY | June 18 | | MAJOR McCALL and 5 Officers including D.A.D.O.S. with 5 Motor Cars proceed to FOLKESTONE for BOULOGNE. | |
| " | 19 | | C.R.S.C. 106044 (O) d/ 18th June, 1916, regarding D.A.D.G. Stores which should be sent in Vans in place of the 74 wagons returned. | |
| " | 22 | 3.30 p.m. | Divisional Headquarters entrained WARMINSTER Railway Station - Arrived SOUTHAMPTON DOCKS 5.55p.m. S.S. PANCRAS left Docks at 8 p.m. | |
| | 23 | 8 a.m. | Arrived Havre.   2/13th Lon. Regt. to MONTS EN TERNOIS - 2/14th Lond. Regt. to BUNEVILLE. | |
| | 24 | 4 p.m. | Divl. Headquarters left HAVRE - 2/13th Lon. Regt.- PENIN - 2/14th - AVERDOINGT - 2/15th MONTS EN TERNOIS - Pioneers - TERNAS | |
| | 25 | 12.15 | Arrived ST. POL and proceeded to FLERS - CHATEAU DE FLERS. 2/13th Battn - ECOIVRES, 2/14th Battn.- MAROEUIL, 2/15th - PENIN, 2/16th ABERDOINGT, 2/17th ECOIVRES (FLERS), Pioneers from TERNAS to LOUEZ & ACQ. | |
| | 26 | | 2/13th, MONT ST ELOI, 2/14th MAROEUIL, 2/15th MAROEUIL, 2/16th ECOIVRES, 2/17th PENIN, 2/18th ABERDOINGT, 2/19th CROISETTE, 2/20th BLANGERMONT, 3/3rd & 2/4th to LOUEZ & MAROEUIL (1/3 on 25th) | |
| | 27 | | H.Q. 179th Bde. from PENIN to ECOIVRES, 2/17th to ACQ, 2/18th to ACQ & MONT ST ELOI, Remainder 180th Bde. to PENIN, 181st to CHELERS from Railway Station ST. POL & PETIT HOUVAIN? 300th R.F.A. Bde. to LAESSET and ACQ and 305rd R.F.A. to ACQ & CAPELLE FERMONT. | |
| | 28 | 8 a.m. | Divl. Hd.Qrs. to VILLERS CHATEL, 1/6th Fld. Coy. to MONT ST ELOI, Hd.Qrs.Coy. A.S.C. to HAUTE AVESNES, 2/21st & 2/22nd Battns. to LOUEZ and MAROEUIL. | |
| | 29 | | D.A.C. arrived ST. POL proceeded ST MICHEL SURTERNOIS. | |
| | 30 | | 2 Companies 2/19th to BOIS DE BRAY & BOIS DE ALLEUX. | |

Phils[?]
A.A.G.
6th Div.

1 July 1916

Army Form C. 2118

60th London Division

# WAR DIARY
or
## INTELLIGENCE SUMMARY
(Erase heading not required.)

Instructions regarding War Diaries and Intelligence Summaries are contained in F.S. Regs., Part II. and the Staff Manual respectively. Title Pages will be prepared in manuscript.

1916

| Place | Date | Hour | Summary of Events and Information | Remarks and references to Appendices |
|---|---|---|---|---|
| VILLERS CHATEL | 1st July | | 3 Brigade Machine Gun Companies which arrived in PENIN & CHELERS area on 30th, detraining at TANCRES moved up to 51 Divisional AREA | Th Rn |
| | | | 2/4 Field Ambulance from MAIZIERES to 51 Divisional Area | |
| | 2nd | | Wire Cutters 832 received for issue | |
| | 3rd | | Div. Gas Helmets completed & issued | |
| | 4th | 6 pm | 1/1 & 1/2 Light Trench Mortar Batteries from LIGNY St FLOCHEL to ECOIVRES and ETRUN Blankets received and issued – mounted troops and A.S.C. to Infantry Divisions having greatcoats issued | Tn |
| | | | 2 Companies 2/19 L. Batt. from PENIN area to 51st Div. area — 2/20 London Batt. from CHELERS | |
| | 5th | | area to 51 Divisional area | |
| | | | 1 Batt. Highland Div. from 51st Div. Area to SAVY by arrangement with Corps. | Ph |
| | 6th | | 3 Medium Trench Mortar Batteries from LIGNES school to 51. Div. Area | |
| | | | 9/23 L Batt. from CHELERS Area (VILLERS BRULIN) to 51 Div Area | |
| | | | 2/24 L Batt. from CHELERS to ST Div. area | |
| | | | D.A.C. 60 L. Div. from St MICHAEL SUR TERNOISE to CAMBLIGNEUL | Ph |
| | | | Hd Qr Co A.S.C. 60 L. Div. 1 Sec. from TANCRES to SAVY — 1 Section of same company | |
| | | | from SAVY to HAUTE AVISNES | |
| | | | No 3 Co. A.S.C. 60 Div Train from DOFFINE FERMES to HAUTE AVISNES | |
| | | | Hd Qs 180 I. BRIGADE from PENIN to SAVY by arrangement with the Corps | |
| | | | 50th Mins R.A. as reinforcement | |

Army Form C. 2118.

60th London Division
**WAR DIARY**
or
**INTELLIGENCE SUMMARY.**
(Erase heading not required.)

WO/1916

| Place | Date | Hour | Summary of Events and Information | Remarks and references to Appendices |
|---|---|---|---|---|
| VILLERS CHATEL | 7th July | | 9/18 L Bat'n fm 51st Division and Area to Villers BRULIN Received OS 63 d/7.7.16 — XVII Order N° 165 10th W'g Pens'rs ffrs received & issued Arrd fm Etrun. From fm TANGRES-Sm- 18 Off'rs & RA as reinforcements | R |
| " | 8 " | | | R |
| " | 9th " | | 2/21 L. Bat'n - from 51st Div. Area to CHELERS | R |
| " | " " | | 1 Offer RCA in reinforcement 4 Officers 2/114 LiReg'l in reinforcements | R |
| " | 10 " | | Guns N° 7 Div'l Tight S'n received — 21 OR to RA reinforcements received | R |
| " | 11 " | | 2/16 VILLERS BRULIN to Mt St ELOY — 22 OR to RA reinforcements ***** OR fm 2/18 received | R |
| " | 12 " | | 2/15 Bat'n to BRAY 100th Field Helmets received & issued having Rifle etc 4 stores | R |
| " | 13 " | | 181st Infantry Brigade to ETRUN — 135 OR to RA — 6 Officers & for 2/114 — 3 OR fm 2/15 | R |
| " | " " | | 180th Infantry Brigade to Mt St ELOY 2000 Steel Helmets received | R |
| " | " " | | 5th Field Ambulance to HAUTE AVESNES 2/21st from CHELERS to ETRUN and forward | R |
| Hermaville HERMAVILLE | 14 " | | Billets for RA + Battalions nrphngrqot HERMAVILLE - TAKEN over from 51st Division Divisional Hd Q's moved to HERMAVILLE - TAKEN over from FORWARD Area | R |
| " | 15 " | | RA Brigades at BETHONSART and TANCQUES to FORWARD Area 2 Companies Divisional Train to HAUTE AVISNES 130 R to RA + Batt'n in reinforcements 1500 Steel Helmets received and distributed D.a.C. from CAMBLIGNEUL to FRAVENT CAPELLE | R |
| " | 16 " | | 2 Officers and 11 OR as reinforcements from Infantry Branch 38 OR to RA. | R |
| " | 17 " | | 3 Death sentences 3 men 181 Inf B°. — Predn fm Montgomerie | R |
| " | 18 " | | NS Inspection of troop of 2 I.C. Div into Corps Advanced party 2 RHA. I.C. Div arrived 20 Other Reinforcement for Infantry Battalion received = attached — Amendment A.O. S/1222 etc | R |
| " | 19 " | | 37 2. ORochns fm 180 + 181 Brigade | R |

# WAR DIARY
## 6 London Division
## INTELLIGENCE SUMMARY

Army Form C. 2118

*(Erase heading not required.)*

Instructions regarding War Diaries and Intelligence Summaries are contained in F.S. Regs., Part II. and the Staff Manual respectively. Title Pages will be prepared in manuscript.

| Place | Date | Hour | Summary of Events and Information | Remarks and references to Appendices |
|---|---|---|---|---|
| HERMAVILLE | 20 July | | 1. Cavalry Divisional Troops moved into Hermaville area — 2 Platoons of 2/25 Bn. | On |
| " | 21 July | | 6 men O.R. reinforcements & 35 O.R. Cyclist W.Hy — 20 Hrs to 2/14 L.R. | On |
| " | 22 | " | 20 Vigilant Periscopes received — 20 very Pistols received | On |
| " | 23 | " | Grenades — Pennants Binoculars — Blankets received — 2 Lt. A.T. POWELL Camp H/Q attached | On |
| " | 24 | " | 4 Officers R.G. Reinforcements — Telescopes & 2d Drain maps rec'd to Inde 2 Phis | On |
| " | 25 | " | 1 O.R. for R.G. & O.T.R for R.E. Reinforcements — Helmets O.H. received in Shermakey Bag | On |
| " | 26 | " | 20.O.R. to 1 Bn. — 2 Officers for R.A Reinforcements — Khayack Stringers, Rod Knives Persil Signs — O.R.s received & issued in Khayack Shripes | Rn |
| " | 27 | " | No phenomena 12 8 Officers R.A. & turns in 28" — Received Trpedes, Synphones — Bren Belts ammunition — Lamps Electric Torch — Sam hanues & saddlery — Sep. | On |
| " | 28 | " | Capt DFW & Capt. MEADE attached to Div STfF Lift for Saverne — 1 Officer to Royal Sandhurst Bn under orders from XVII Corp — Signal O.R.s — RSRs Smith & Wesson for In. S hanne — 10/Hun LT G.T HELLICAR previously reported missing by 2/20 L. Bn. now reported Killed | On |
| " | 29 | | 10/Hun killed 2/20 Bn." LT T GARDIVER | Rn |
| " | 30 | " | 1420 A.H. for Helmets Received — Pistols Holsters 14 received | Rn |
| " | 31 | " | Relief of 1 Cavalry Brigade Troops in Brav Area — Marning their 8 maps for 18" M.S.C. units arrived — Distillers Spring — Shells for Bodies — Carviens Magpers — Div Sight 1 — received & issued | On |

Phil. Smyth Lt.
G. S. G/20 6.2 Devon.

Secret.

Vol 3

War Diary

A & Q Branch, H.Q. 60th (London) Divn.

From August 1st 1916 to August 31st 1916.

Army Form C. 2118.

60th Division

WAR DIARY
or
INTELLIGENCE SUMMARY.
(Erase heading not required.)

Instructions regarding War Diaries and Intelligence Summaries are contained in F.S. Regs., Part II. and the Staff Manual respectively. Title pages will be prepared in manuscript.

| Hour, Date, Place | Summary of Events and Information | Remarks and references to Appendices |
|---|---|---|
| HERMAVILLE 1915 Aug 1st | 2/Lt W A READ - accidentally wounded at 1st Bn Brigade Bombing School. A/Sgt Wheat & 899Pte received - Crew (Breach) 1000Pte. Grenade Carriers 300 - Varnish Sponges - Received. | Pn |
| " Aug 2nd | 2/Lt J. TYNDALL 3/16th R. wounded - Bicycles & Bicycle Tyres received & issued. | Pn |
| " Aug 3rd | 111 OR received at Reinforcement Camp for 180 & 181 1st Brigades. Bicycles & R.E. - In Reserve. - Hyposulphite - Conning Pins - etc - Haversacks - Emers Dressings Pkts, AR Outers, water Sfg Ans. - A few loose pistols received - 2 Officers & 16 ORs Reinforcements arrived - 300 Steel Helmets received. | Pn |
| " Aug 4th | Pte AE Travers 18 ...... Private ALFRED SMITH and W G HUBBLE wounded. To Military Medal in immediate reward. | Pn |
| " Aug 5th | Lt C WALLIS 2/16 2 Batt. and 2/Lt D F EVANS 2/24 2 Batt. to make 1 Officer & Sgt to School of Cookery - 2 Officers & Sgt. to School of Cookery Dunkirk QS. | Pn |
| Aug 6th | 2/Lt A J DAVIS 2/18 2 Batt. Wounded ──── 1 Officer to 2/20 1 Officer to 2/22 1 Rpt to reinforcement 2 OR to Signal Co. ──── Sick Visitors - Clothing - Carriers Arm " received by SADOS for issue ──── Authority received to hold 6800 iron Rations in Reserve. ──── Corps Commander awarded MILITARY MEDAL to Private SMITH and HUBBLE 2/20 2 Batt. | Pn |
| Aug 7th | Received 2-18pr carriages with air recuperators. 12-13pr guns to ANTI-AIRC. 1 Sister Nurse - Helmets & Valentia anti gas - Returned & issued. | Pn |
| Aug 8th | Received to President of Round Visit (informal) All concerned informed. Rendezvous at ........ Military of Signals District of Manchester Hants - passengers L. Coy 3rd/30 Bn. for Signals Proc. issued - 20mm aged ....... Lt EDMUNDS.R.A., L.F.FLINT 2/23 Batt. Officers & SMs in Times to Round Visit - Round Visit of J. Elvi 3.45 to 4.30pm. | Pn |
| Aug 9th | Altercation in Times to Round Visit - A/Lt Munford with 1 Bn. 2/14 2/17 2/21 2/24 arrived. A/Capt WILLS 2/13 2 Batt. 185. Machy Gun Coy 179 Bngde. Lieut W READ and Corpl WILLS 2/13 2 Batt. and LIEUT FLINT 2/23 2 Batt. to report for immediate return. | Pn |

Forms C. 2118/10

(9 29 6) W 4141—463 100,000 9/14 H W V

Page 2

**WAR DIARY**
or
**INTELLIGENCE SUMMARY.**
(Erase heading not required.)

Army Form C. 2118.

| Hour, Date, Place | Summary of Events and Information | Remarks and references to Appendices |
|---|---|---|
| HERMAVILLE Aug. 10th | Reinforcements 1 Officer & 2/24 L.Bn — 6 O.R. for 179 & 181 M.G.C. | Pm |
| " Aug. 11th 1916 | Corp. G.B. WILLS 2/23 L.B. wounded. Capt. BARCLAY H.Q. & Capt. DAVID DEVIS 2/13 Rfl. & Brenan Team & Capt. SPIGMON 2/24, Return of Tough Rifle Scavvers Pm L'TYLER — CAPT DAVID DEVIS 2/13 Rft & Brenan Team vy Capt. SPIGMON 2/24. Return of Reinforcements 1 Officer from 2/2 L. Ray — R.S.C. — 2 O.R. — 1 R.E. Officer — LT. KILLINGBECK 2/3 C. — Killed. Pm 2/Lt W.TEMPLE 2/17 L Battn wounded | |
| Aug 12 1916 | Received Periscope N° 9 — 4 — Sprayers Machetype 30 — Horse Clippers etc Returned | Pm |
| | 2 O.R. for Colychest C. — Major Sir H. DUNBAR attached to H.Q. 2/13 went to ENGLAND to attend to Board | Pm |
| Aug 13 | 1/Lt E.B. BROWN 2/16 L.Reg wounded Rec'd Vickers parts Compressed Pets — Cloth for making Signals & Aeroplanes | |
| Aug 14 | C.O.R. Ladder — Horse Clippers etc. Reinforcements 1 Officer 2/14 — 3 Officers 2/15 — 10 Officers 2/15 — 2 Officers 2/21 — O.R 1 O.R. 2/10 — 15 O.R.s 14 R.R. Pm | |
| Aug 15 | sub Stoves & Equipment received & issued | |
| | Returned 1 Officer to 2/16 — O.R. major for 2/15 — | Pm |
| | LT ELLIOT and 2/LT MORRIS of 2/20 Wounded — French acting Interpreter Officer 179/B.A. — Transferred C. — 2/6 R.A | |
| | Received N° 7 Dial Sight 2 — Bicycles Infantry pattern — Capt. 2 Machineguns 1 Acting Interpreter 2/22 1 R.E. Officer from Corps Machine Gun Office WHEELER 2/13 T.R. — Cnr to Corp. SMITH — Pt. HUDGELL 2/B 2/2 Ray | Pm |
| Aug 16 | Reinforcements 2/16 L.B 2 — 2/15 — 1 | |
| | 2/Lt WILSON 2/14 L.B. wounded — Reg G.S. waggon for Tuckers C. etc. | Pm |
| Aug 17th | LT A.S. FORBES — 181 M.G.C. Wounded — Bn 72 — Bicycles parts etc received and issued | Pm |
| Aug 18 | Reinforcements 2/13 O.R 5 — 2/14 Officers 1 OR 43 — 2/15 OR 3 — 2/16 OR 2 2/17 — OR 4 2/18 — OR 64 — 2/19 OR 3 2/20 OR 3 — 2/21 — OR 4 — 2/22 — OR 99 2/23 — Officers 1, OR 2 — 2/24 — R.G.A.C. Officers 1 — O.R.J Reinforcements accounted. 1/N Officer 2/Rifles Leaves Commenced. — 650 Steel Helmets Received. Cards leaves from Corps Is. Forbes/C.2118/10 | Pm |

60 London Division
Page 3

# WAR DIARY
## INTELLIGENCE SUMMARY
Army Form C. 2118

*(Erase heading not required.)*

Instructions regarding War Diaries and Intelligence Summaries are contained in F.S. Regs., Part II. and the Staff Manual respectively. Title Pages will be prepared in manuscript.

| Place | Date | Hour | Summary of Events and Information | Remarks and references to Appendices |
|---|---|---|---|---|
| HERMAVILLE | Aug 19 | | Infantry Drafts advised on Aug 18th arrived except drafts for 2/22 & 98 infs & or 299 O.R. 10 Officers for 2/17 extra arrival. Guns completed in line except on 4 Stokes & 19 extra ammunition. Vickers guns in front & Stokes parts received also Gen Lewis Charles from — Bed detail for Trench Mortars (4) received. Issued | Ph. |
| " | 20" | | Reinforcements 3 O.R. per A.S.C. arrived on 18/9 MGC — All Guns & handlers to Line. Received 750 Steel helmets & various small trench mortar Ordnance Stores | Ph. |
| " | 21" | | 16 men arrived on 1/6 H.R.E. — LIEUT F.S. MACKENZIE 2/15 L.Bat" wounded. Periscope N°9 (3) — Picketting gear. Machine gun fire ?? — Brigade Bytes received. | Ph. |
| " | 22" | | Reinforcements 1 Officer cards for 2/13 2/15 2/19, 2 Officers for 2/20 — 1 Gunner Inf", 1 Corporal in R.E. — 30 R.A.M.C. & 9 Coys. 1 Officer & 2 O.R. CARVER & Dragoons Adieu — 1 Officer 2/19 Reg", 2nd Lt C.E. CREES wounded. Bicycles, Air Artillery (15) Vermont Sprayers — Cycling Holding Cooker — Periscopic Compasses received & issued | Ph. |
| " | 23 | | Reinforcement 16 men for 2/20 L.Reg" — 60 15 pf June & 9 October — premature in bore. 850 Steel helmets received. Brigade data for other in Lamps Godfrey 3rd & 4th tops — Supplement in dies for type railway — C in C amended ... Cross. LIEUT READ 2/19 Bat" and LIEUT FLINT 2/23 Reg" 1 — 16pf fr p 300 R.D.A — Signalling Telescopes — Howitzers received & issued | Ph. |
| " | 24 | | 1 Officer reinforcement for 2/17 L.Reg". | Ph. |
| " | 25 | | Bicycles for R.E. (1) — Blades — Periscope N°9 — Road netting — Signalling Telescopes received. | Ph. |
| " | 26 | | Reinforcements Officers 2, Other Ranks 15 for 2/15 L.Bat", 1 Officer 2/20 — 1 Man & 18 O.R. per 2/23 L. Reg" Dog spoon Tamps in 2517 — Ingersoll — Periscopes — Compasses Prismatic — Grenade Carriers 350 — Received & Issued | Ph. Ph. |
| " | 27 | | Capt J.W.A. CRAIG wounded (since died), 2nd Lt J.A.C. HASSLACHER 2/20 L.Reg", Wounded. Reinforcement 1 Officer for 2/23 — 15 O.R. for 2/15 — 30 R.A. R.E. & C. 240 Reg" for 2/23. J.B.C. & A. A.D.S.S./Forms/C.2118. 1 Vickers & Spare receives from 180 A.G.C. | Ph. |

1875 W. W593/826 1,000,000 4/15

60" London Div n
Part 4

# WAR DIARY or INTELLIGENCE SUMMARY

Army Form C. 2118

(Erase heading not required.)

Instructions regarding War Diaries and Intelligence Summaries are contained in F. S. Regs, Part II. and the Staff Manual respectively. Title Pages will be prepared in manuscript.

| Place | Date | Hour | Summary of Events and Information | Remarks and references to Appendices |
|---|---|---|---|---|
| HERMAVILLE | Aug 28 | | Reinforcement for 2/16 – OR 48 – for 2/20 – OR 27 | Th |
| | | | 1 Offr & 1 OR 45 out of action — Parascope & fire Petrs received | |
| " | Aug 29 | | Reinforcements for 2/15 – 5 Offrs – 2/17 3 Offrs – 2/22 – 4 Offrs | Th |
| | | | 2/20 – 5 OR left at Albertville + abt 28' arrived — 1.OR for R.G.A. (Siege) + 1 for Intelligence | |
| | | | Lt Col. R. M. BIRKETT wounded. 2/17 Bat" — | |
| | | | 8 Brigden for Ra — Saddler y — Bar. R.Ruelrs received allowance | |
| | | | Letters received that all surplus personnel of R.A. Sen Brigade on reorganization O.R.A.F.A. | |
| | | | Horse Depot — Offrs & arms' Indus. & H.Q. | |
| Aug 30 | | Reinforcement 1 Offr for 181 B.f.C. 4 OR for R.A.7 Bat – 4 OR for 181 B.f.C. – 1 for P.E. | Th |
| | | | 1st Lieut M LANE 2/20 L.B. Wounded — | |
| Aug 31st | | Reinforcement for Trances 2 Offrs — 60 L.Div. Train OR.4 | Bn |
| | | | 2/Lt W.A. WILLIAMS 2/19 L.Ry. Wounded, 1 Lewis gun complete for 2/16 Bat" in | Th |
| | | | exc A. 5" Howitzer received & Battery 303 Brig" — | |
| | | | is place on damaged by Shell fire | |
| | | | Corps MDtg notice removed from Divisional area of 1st Indian Cavalry Brigade — attached | |
| | | | Troops & 1st Squadron R.E. + Hqr R.H.A. Brigade 1st I.C. Div. will move later. Sinai | |
| | | | working Parties + 1st Sqdn R.E. & I.C. Div. weapons and firearms & report Since — No | |
| | | | relief | |

Malcolm Porter
A.A. & g.md
60 L Division

# WAR DIARY / INTELLIGENCE SUMMARY

**1916** — 61st London Division — Army Form C. 2118

| Place | Date | Hour | Summary of Events and Information | Remarks and references to Appendices |
|---|---|---|---|---|
| HERMAVILLE | SEP 1st | | 72 Headcovers for Lewis Machine Guns received — Preference & M. form 2/4 received | |
| | 2nd | | Reinforcements 1 Officer for 2/15 — 2/19 — 2/21 — 2/22 ———— 1 Officer = 6th W T CHISHOLM 2/25 Regt wounded (Sheedud & wounded in Hospital) —— 550 Steel Helmets — Packer Bros Carpenters Bicycle parts & Lewis Gun parts — (5th Battn'n needs for Lewis Gun machine received) — N.5473 2/Corp. BRADLEY 2/23 Batt'n awarded the D.C. Medal. (XVIII Corps W'ar. A 6/107 of death) Orders from 3rd Army — 61 Div Cable Co. will move to Avelimy 4/9/16 | |
| | 3rd | | MAJOR OGILBY reported his arrival to Division. Command of the 2/13 L. Regt nu 2/Th DUNSMORE Wounded (shell-shock) —— 32nd F.H. FROST 2/17 2nd Regt wounded 6/2 Officer & 1/Hants Regt Regt Div Arer —— 2 Gun Holdh Auts 1863 arrived for persons | |
| | 4th | | Reinforcements 1 Offr to 2/5 M.G.Brigade —— 2/L D.A.LEWIS 180 machine guns returned Helmet. Picq. Penisch W 16. Signalling Panics received | |
| | 5th | | Reinforcements 5 Offrs to 6th Div Accnt. 1 for Div —— 1 Officer for RAMC —— 1 = 16 ST from Reinforcements of 2/4 Sattn Indoors & ext. for letters —— Rides for Pigs — Peniscopes W 15 Periscopes 4 — 1 Bicycles returned | |
| | 6th | | Reinforcements 10 Offrs to each of 2/nd.y Batt'n 2 — 2/13 — 2/15 — 2/17 — 2/20 — 2/24 — 2 Offrs for 2/20 Reg 1 Officer for 180 M.G.C. —— 131 M.G.C. 2 — 180 M.G.C. 4 — Reinforcements O.R 1/6 Yorks — M.T.&S.C 1 — Carrier Groom & Knapsacks Bridges steel tube & Reell 1/2yd (1 1/8" — Carrier Groom & Knapsacks Bridges steel tube Move 2.3 Batt'n of 3rd Division on from OTU' area report just cancelled 122 Ex G.C — | |
| | 7th | | Reinforcements 1 Officer 1 for RE Signals — O.R 1 ment. 2/14 2/17 2/23 W.L Reserves Vais. transport — Boots — Box Respirators — Periscopes — Binoculars | |
| | 8th | | Offrs Reinforcements 1 for Div Signal C = 2 O R for 2/14 — 10 R for 2/19 & 2/20 Batt' — 1 for A.S.C. Wounded Capt "PICKTHORN 2/15 Batt" and Major GORDON GILL 2/24 Regt 19 Scyer stores received —— RGA Reservations rec'd | |

Army Form C. 2118

# WAR DIARY
## INTELLIGENCE SUMMARY
*(Erase heading not required.)*

Instructions regarding War Diaries and Intelligence Summaries are contained in F. S. Regs., Part II. and the Staff Manual respectively. Title Pages will be prepared in manuscript.

| Place | Date | Hour | Summary of Events and Information | Remarks and references to Appendices |
|---|---|---|---|---|
| HERMAVILLE | Sept 9 | | 1 Officer reinft. reinforcement from 2/17, 2/19, 2/20, 2/24 — 52 H/phosphere reserve — 17 Verekers from trenches. Periscopes N.5 = 4 — short reports for Brigades, Divisions & Corps | Ga |
| | 10 | | Division allotment prepared to 1st Army. 6.39 18pr in at return (8 with 10m & 1 under repair in gun position) — Pioneer Batn delivered to Escoivres & handed to A.O.G. — Periscope N.3 = N.9 — Periscope N.18 — Autoclave Sterilises & Hypo Received. 100 steel helmets | Ga |
| | 11 | | 6 Officers wounded 1/Lt H.S. ROBINSON 2/21st Btn, (Canadian Scottish) xxx Division turned into Autoclave Sterilises & Hypo Periscopes N.5 — 80 1 Batn. S.L. Regt (Pioneers) xxx Division turned into Autoclave Sterilises & Hypo received 1st Bn. 3 L. Regt (Pioneers) Light Siege 1760 generators Autoclave PH 927. Autoclave PH.g 241 | Pa |
| | 12 | | 2/Lt B. PEATFIELD and 2/Lt G.F. THOMPSON 9/15 2 Battns wounded. Reinforcements Officers 3/15 4/16 2/17 2/20 1/Lt 2/21 1/Lt 2/23 — Other ranks 2 pr R.E. Yorks 1st Reserve. 2 Sections T.M. B. XXX Division at MARŒUIL. Periscopes N.15 (3) Periscopes N.9 (7) — Bucketclothes Brother & Chepterel, Jones, Lemon gone. | Pa |
| | 13 | | 8 Officers killed 2/Lt G.T. KINROSS & 2/Lt F.A. THEW Herbert SLUI (280,000) — Bucketclothe dye — pots for Lemon Jones into reserve 210 9th R.E. (xxx Division) moved into ECOIVRES — 3 Sec. Turned in 4 & Lime | Ga |
| | 14 | | Reinforcements Officers 1 ea 2/15, 2/16, 2/19, 2/20 — 1 Chaplain to 180 I. Brigade — Gas Stoves — Helmets PH.9 4757 received. 3/Lt A. HAYNES — R.Q. wounded — Helmets PH.G 4757 received — 17 Bn. LIVERPOOL REGIMENT (xxx Div.) to ECOIVRES — The 278 R.G.C. 14 Fr. Arty. A.A. Battery — change at Officer 1 Sec. 62 Brigade to relieve 1 Sec. 40 Bde y. — 83 A.A. Sec/110 Light Gas. | Pa |
| | 15 | | 2 Sec 9/26. 253 Turning C. R.E. ECOIVRES | Pa |
| | 16 | | Reinforcements 6 Ranks 1/17 3/13 — 9 Fr 3/15 2 Cpls 3/18 — 15 Pr 3/21 — steel helmets 532 stock Helmets PH.G 750 — went impreg in autoclave Resuscitate in 180 It.Bde. Other 3 receive fire Tents 6 + 4 xxx Division to leave Div formed Ogres 1m — 18 pr gun back in action making up 47 — | Ga |

1875 Wt. W593/826 1,000,000 4/15 J.B.C. & A. A.D.S.S./Forms/C. 2118.

# WAR DIARY / INTELLIGENCE SUMMARY

Army Form C. 2118

60 London Division

| Place | Date | Hour | Summary of Events and Information | Remarks and references to Appendices |
|---|---|---|---|---|
| HERMAVILLE | Sept. | 17 | Reinforcements — OR — 2/13 — 3 — 2/14 — 4 — 2/17 — 3 — 2/18 — 5 — 2/19 — 8 — 2/20 — 9 — 2/21 — 7 — 2/22 — 2 — 2/23 — 16 — 2/24 — 3<br>1 Officer for 3rd L. Regt — Lewis Guns & Mags rec (48) Passed Ord No 26 - (4) Lewis Guns Parties returned<br>G.S. XVII Corps G.15 - 16.9.16 — 1st Divist - 17 Magic Suns (Armrs) 266 2nd C.M.E. — From 1st Pr Pr 17 Corps 17.9.16 by<br>Road to Ecoivres — Army Comm Letter (II Corps) Groups of 7 MGC 2.87 Arms returned to Division | OR |
| " | " | 18 | Reinforcement - 1 Officer for 2/24 Batt — OR — 35 for 2/19 — 8 Pr RE Companies 3 for 1858 N.S.C.<br>850 Blankets received authority for issue from OC DCS | OR |
| " | " | 19 | Reinforcement - 7 Officers for 2/13 L Batt — OR — 3 for 2/13 — 1 for R9A —<br>Troops of 32nd Div ordered to move into D Divisions Area on 17 - 18th Sept - now ordered to HQ Ecoivres & ACS<br>Pioneers in RE & ACG — Details of Ecoivres from where they moved up on 18th. 32 Div DAC also ordered<br>to move from Co - to region 32 Div tomorrow. 10 Officers of 3rd OTT 9 Divison 1st S.A. Inf'y moved into Divison | OR |
| " | " | 20 | 300 Blankets received — line HE 13 & HE D 1 offr horses received by 2ndLieutenant — Gun Buster (Army) issued and Practised<br>authorized scale — Heavy Guns of A & 2/4/5 Howitzer Battery & Lewis Guns Buttie received | OR |
| " | " | 21 | Reinforcement 3 Officers for 2/13 Batt — 1 Officer for 2/12 L.N. Lancs Pioneers<br>1 Officer 2/19 Lt E.SCHONFIELD killed — Armoured Carriers recommend —<br>Motor Mach Gun Battery recommend GS Div Order No 78 9/20. 9/16 Mar D 9th Div note to be returned by 24 Div<br>R.2 Lt G.E.THOMSON 2/1157 Regt recommend DS.0 - Lt B. PEATFIELD 2/15 awarded for Myfrs Gallantry in action on 11.11.15<br>OTR Inoculation 6/4R 2 for 2/13 1 for 2/14 1 for 2/15 3 for 2/17 4 for 2/20 1 for RA | OR |
| " | " | 22 | Blankets received 1200 — from Bodri 760 Paris | OR |
| " | " | 23 | Reinforcements 8/15 — 7 OR — 2/16 7 OR — 1 Officer 2/2 Lt H.C. BULTON 2/14 L.R received<br>Branches and Received 300 — Ground coats 1240 — Blankets 1800 received<br>4 Officers 37 OR HQ Heavy A Group St A, St Eloi — 3 Mins 100 OTP Sig Rectry R9 A St Bray<br>1 Off 30 OR 4 Corps Cyclist Batt A.Maunoil — Lieut J.C. RAFTER 2/20 L Regt awarded Military Cross | OR |
| " | " | 24 | Reinforcements 1 Officer for 2/16 — 2/20 — R3 A — 70 O Rgrs 2/14 L Regt — 30 Mens from<br>2 nd Lieutenancy Button<br>1 Officer 2 Lt F.WILSON 180 MGC accidentally wounded 32 ORs Blankets Received<br>Head 52 Siege Battery 2nd in M/St ELOI. G Donetson M/St ELOI | OR BRAY |

# WAR DIARY or INTELLIGENCE SUMMARY

Army Form C. 2118

60 London Division

| Place | Date | Hour | Summary of Events and Information | Remarks and references to Appendices |
|---|---|---|---|---|
| Hermaville | Sept 25 | | Reinforcements 30 OR for 1/6 7a C. RE — 1 OR for 3/3 9a C. RE — 1 OR for 303 R.F.A. 2/Lt E.D.R. PINKERTON 2/15 L. Regt. wounded — 2/Lt C.R. TOWNEND and 2/Lt E.H. TIDDY 2/21 L. Regt. joined | |
| " | 26 | | Reinforcements 1 Officer for each of following Units 2/17 LR, 2/19 LR, 2/21 LR, 2/23 LR. 10 pw. from Entrenching Batt. to 2/17 Regt. Reinforcements O.R. 20 t. 2/22 L. Regt — 5 H.D.G.C. — Staff Notice 943 — Magazine Carriers S'38 — Conference Post Trench Mortars & keeping from Reserve. Corps Commander presented D.C.M. ribbon to 1 N.C.O. 2/23 & 2 N.C.O.s Parted Ribbons & June 3/15— 2 am 3/19 3 am 3/20. | |
| " | 27 | | Reinforcements 1 Officer for 3/16 LR, 2/17 LR — 3/13 LR — 3/22 LR & 2/24 LR and 150 M. Gun Co. Reinforcements O.R. 2/15 LR — & 3/16 LR, 2/17 LR 4 — 3/18 LR 7  2/19 LR, 3/20 LR 2, 2/21 LR 3, 2/24 LR 1. R.A.L 7. O.R. 5 for 3/18 — 6 for 3/15 — 3 for 3/16 | |
| " | 28 | 11 pm 2/15 – 8 pm 22 | Reinforcements — Officers 1 for 3/16 LR 1 for 3/15 LR 1 for 3/22 LR — Receives Trench Mortars 2" four — 3" one | |
| " | 29 | | Reinforcement — Officers 1 transfer of Machine Guns Recruits 3/15 — 3/15 — 3/20 — 3/24 — 101 M.G.Co. 5 O.R. 1 posted Invalided to 2 Cap'n 1 Riflemen 3/16 L. Regt — Pars v Ron N.Y received 10 pw. wounded LIEUT T.G.C. COGGIN 3/14 L. Regt. | |
| " | 30 | | Attachments — Pars. m.d. Vickers Guns received — Carrier 3 G.S. — 13 x 18 ph received | |

1.X.1916

Thos R. John
A.A. & Q.M.S. 60 London Div.

Secret.

Vol 5

War Diary

60th Division.

A.Q. Branch.

From 1st Oct. 1916 to 31st Oct. 1916.

**Army Form C. 2118**

**WAR DIARY** or **INTELLIGENCE SUMMARY**

60th London Division
1916
Secret

Instructions regarding War Diaries and Intelligence Summaries are contained in F.S. Regs., Part II. and the Staff Manual respectively. Title Pages will be prepared in manuscript.

(Erase heading not required.)

| Place | Date | Hour | Summary of Events and Information | Remarks and references to Appendices |
|---|---|---|---|---|
| HERMAVILLE | OCTOBER 1st | | Reinforcements Officers – Our. Breach of Nursing Regiment 9/16 – 9/18 – 9/23 – 9/24  Stores for R.E. Companies 10 OR/m 2/20 I.R.  1 Officer 2/2nd E.A. CLARKE 2/20 L Regt wounded | R |
| | 2nd | | Reinforcement Nurs Officers R.A.M.C. – 5 ORR to 180 M.G.C. – 10 ORR 166 A.G.C.  170 Siege Battery R.G.A. withdrawn from Line – Nagasaki Armoured 43 H.Q. Grps. | Ph |
| | 3rd | | Reinforcement Officers 2/17 = 2  2/19 = 3  2/20 = 3  2/22 = 3  2/23 = 1 R.A.M.C. = 2  2 Military Batmen arrested  1 N.C.O. 2/5 a 3/14 L. Regt (London Scottish) | Ph |
| | 4th | | Reinforcement Officers 1 to each Bttn  Bttn 2/17 – 2/19 – 2/22  2/20 – Sanitarium – Barrows Ludington 2/3 R.S  Received Historic 7th – South Staffs – Bgr French Learnings – Infantry Musketry Course  2nd HIPWELL 7/16 awarded Military Cross | Ph |
| | 5th | | Reinforcement Officers 2/10 1 2/17 1 wounded Lt MacBroom (RE-attached) 1/6 Loud R.  1 Offr 2/20 Lond R | M+ |
| | 6th | | Reinforcement Lt C.D. Wells 60 Tnwt  Wounded 2/16 AP LANE 1/14 LOND R  9/18 F.P.J BULPIN York R replaced on ADC in Gee | |
| | 7th | | Reinforcement 2 Offrs 1 Sgt for ship 2/12 2/14 after 9/14 Lond R wounded 3 OR  302 Bn RPA | |
| | 8th | | Reinforcement 2 Offrs/m 2/13, Equal R, 1 Offr/m 2/19 Lond R | |
| | 9th | | 1 4.5" Howitzer and toll in (manufacture in Gore) | |
| | 10th | | Wounded CAPT COLMER, Lt HAYFORD, 2/5 ARNOLD and WESTON of 1/22 Bn (Raid Grenade)  10.5th Hamdled German Grenades received for instructional use  Reinforcement 9/2/ DUNPHY 9/18 Lond from Hicks all of 2/18 Lond Bn.  Award of Million | |
| | 11th | | Wounded Lt BROWN, 2/15 Kimberley & Gurling.  Killed/m Dolby 9/16 & Sgt Albert 9/14 G  Lt Cross Bn to Macfarlane 2/14, 2/15 Dolby 9/16 & 1st Bn to Sgt DEEN 2/14 G | N |

1875. Wt. W593/826. 1,000,000. 4/15. J.B.C. & A. A.D.S.S./Forms/C. 2118.

60 London Division
# WAR DIARY
## or
## INTELLIGENCE SUMMARY
*(Erase heading not required.)*

Army Form C. 2118

Instructions regarding War Diaries and Intelligence Summaries are contained in F.S. Regs., Part II. and the Staff Manual respectively. Title Pages will be prepared in manuscript.

| Place | Date | Hour | Summary of Events and Information | Remarks and references to Appendices |
|---|---|---|---|---|
| HERMAVILLE | Oct 1916 | 12 | Reinforcements 2/13 - OR 10 - 2/14 OR 5 - 2/15 OR 2 - 2/16 Officers 1 - OR 2 - 2/17 OR 4 - 2/18 40 2/20 - 4 2/23 MG 4 OR 3. — Officer killed 2/ Lt SANDERSON. Officers wounded Capt ROSEVEAR and Lt RANGE 2/13 L. Regt Lt MOSER 2/17 L. Regt. — Received Gun Book 840 — Lewis Gun Post OF 4 shows. QF L Pattern. | PM |
|  | " | 13th | Reinforcements Officers out for each Regt various ranks — 2/16 L Regt — 2/18 O.R. (2) — 1/6 L Regt. Passenger Pilot from Berlin 1446 prisoners recovered — Brig. Genl DA COSTA reported for duty in relief of Brig. Genl PARSONS — Railhead changed from to AUBIGNY to FREVIN CAPELLE | PM |
|  | " | 14th | Reinforcements 2/13 L Regt 1 Officer 94 OR — 2/15 L Regt 37/OR 2/18 LR 1 Officer 36/OR — Received from Base 24 prisoners — Very Pistols 1" - 15 1½" - 2 Parisiens | PM |
|  | " | 15 | Reinforcements 1/12 L Devon Regt OR 3 Rec. G.S. 398/1 d/15.8.1916 from "G" arriving from 9.770 d/14.8.16 from XVIII Corps | PM |
|  | " | 16 | Reinforcements 1 Officer 2/16 LR - 1 Man 2/14 2L RB 10 privates 2/20 LR Other Ranks 1/15 LR 2/22 LR 35 - 2/15 LR 29 — LIEUT HIPWELL 2/16 L Regt Killed 2/ Sea Rose 2/23 L R wounded | PM |
|  | " | 17 | Reinforcements OR 2/15-1 - 2/18 - 1 — 2/20 - 3 — 2/25 - 3 — 2/28 2/L RB 2 - 2/27 L R 2 - 3 Received parts for Gun Lewis & for Vickers Extractors & QF 15 pieces 1/6 H. RB 2 — Received parts & cover apron 607. Du: & complete RA Sketchbook No picks received 379 How Battery — Du Trips - 1 — Dec 18 per from L. Sotton, and Partner — | PM |
|  | " | 18 | Reinforcements OR 2/14 - 4 2/15 - 4 — Box Respirators Sml large types Large Box Respirators 110 — Sheep Skin Coats 360 — Leather Jerkins 480 — Helmet Trench Gutters 1104 | OR |

**WAR DIARY**
or
**INTELLIGENCE SUMMARY**
*(Erase heading not required.)*

Army Form C. 2118

| Place | Date | Hour | Summary of Events and Information | Remarks and references to Appendices |
|---|---|---|---|---|
| HERMAVILLE | Oct 19 | 12½ | Reinforcement Officers & Other ranks Received :- 8/9 KR — 1 — 18/19 G.G. 1 — Reinforcements O.R. 3/13 — 3 — 3/14 — 5 — 3/15 — 1 — 3/16 — 2 — 3/19 — 1 3/20 — 3 — 3/21 — 3 — 3/23 — 3 — 3/24 — 3 — — — — — 3 Officers posted from 2 on horse dep. at Rouen. 13.25 — Polo Practice — Reinforcements received by 2nd Batt. — Three horses cast | Pm |
| | 20 | — | 2nd Lieut. C.A. SOUTHIN 2/21 L. Regt. reported. — — Three horses cast to investigate | Pm |
| | 21 | — | two 18 Pounders being overhauled by 1.O.M. 2nd Lt C.B. WARD 2/21 L. Regt. reported — Two 18 Pounders and 3 Stretcher being overhauled by 1.O.M | Pm / Pm |
| | 22 | — | Received the Brigadier's Inspection. Both Lewis Ammn 1455 rounds returned to HAVRE 1 British Hundgun wounded 2/Lt C.F. BURN 1/4 L.R — Three 18 Pounders and 2 Stretcher being overhauled by 1.O.M | Pm |
| | 23 | — | One Officer wounded 2/Lt S.E. JONES 2/14 L.R — Three 18 Pounders being overhauled Three 18 Pr being overhauled by 1.O.M. | Pm |
| | 24 | — | Officers wounded 2/Lt R.F. NORBURY 181 M.G. Co — Three 18 Pounders being overhauled 1.O.M | Pm / Pm |
| | 25 | — | 2/Lt— WOODMAN 8/17 Batt L. Regt. was awarded Military Cross — E Smith SMITH 2/13 Bn L Regt awarded D.C.M — 1 Vickers gun for 179 Brigade rec'd 3 Eighteen Pounders gun being overhauled at 1.O.M | Pm / Pm |
| | 26 | — | Reinforcement — Machine Gun Corporation — Officers 2 — R & M.G. 2 — B. H & G.S. regt HERMAVILLE at 10am and opened at HOUVIN 3rd Army Corps — | Pm |
| HOUVIN | 27 | — | Div' Hd Q. at HOUVIN — Troops (less Artillery) concentrated in that area — | Pm |

**Army Form C. 2118**

Instructions regarding War Diaries and Intelligence Summaries are contained in F.S. Regs., Part II. and the Staff Manual respectively. Title Pages will be prepared in manuscript.

# WAR DIARY
## INTELLIGENCE SUMMARY
*(Erase heading not required.)*

| Place | Date | Hour | Summary of Events and Information | Remarks and references to Appendices |
|---|---|---|---|---|
| FROHEN LE GRANDE | Oct 1916 28th | | DHQ and Troops of 60 Division (less Artillery) moved into FROHEN LE GRANDE and AREA and remained the day. | Thn |
| | 29 | | Reinforcements 1 Officer 40R 1/3/21 — 10R 1/3/21 — 10R 2/3/6 Outfitline — 10R a S.C. Dir HQRS moved into BERNAVILLE and Troops into 10Rs area adjoining. R/Es 3/3/3 Cdn mtd Reg rec'd on 29. x.16. Re-inforcements 2/13 — 4 OR — 2/14 — 1 OR — 2/15 — 2 OR — 2/16 — 10R — 2/17 — 10R — 2/19 — 2 OR — 2/20 — 1OR 2/21 — 3 OR — 2/22 — 1 OR — 2/23 — 3 OR — Pioneers 2 OR. Machine Gun C. 2 OR — 160Th Battery 1 OR Asc 1 OR — Division remained in BERNAVILLE AREA — 2/14 JC. RE. hrs D 13F Corps term | Thn |
| BERNAVILLE | 30 | | | Thn |
| " | 31 | | Division Hd Qs remain in BERNAVILLE and the Division in that area — Orders received that RE Companies return to Divisional Area 4th Army G 3733 d/31.X.1916 regarding further movements received — Adm O.B. 1847 | Thn |

ThusShyle
A.A + Q.M.G
60th Infantry Division

Army Form C. 2118

HQ A.D 60 Vol 6

6th Adm Division
WAR DIARY
or
INTELLIGENCE SUMMARY
(Erase heading not required.)

Instructions regarding War Diaries and Intelligence Summaries are contained in F.S. Regs., Part II. and the Staff Manual respectively. Title Pages will be prepared in manuscript.

| Place | Date | Hour | Summary of Events and Information | Remarks and references to Appendices |
|---|---|---|---|---|
| BERNAVILLE | Nov 1st | | 2/4 Lieut. C. returned to Division — | Tm / Tm |
| AILLE | 2nd | | 9/6 & 3/3 Lieut C. returned to Division | Pm |
| LE HAUT | 3rd | | Division moved into the new area. Div HQ's at AILLY — Arrangements to withdraw the intn from Pioneer Battalion ordered to be known | Pm |
| CLOCHER | 4 | | Orders issued for the return of the Pioneer Bn's to 1st Army area — Orders received to withdraw Pn Machine & 1 Cav't Reserve Park | Pm |
| " | 5 | | DAC completed march to PONT REMY. Pioneers left Division. Notification received of 2nd Ind' Cavalry Reserve Park Division to move into area | Pm |
| " | 6 | | Division HQ today reorganizing & reequipping | Pm |
| " | 7 | | 2nd Indian Cav Division Reserve Park arrived at L'ETOILE & the howitzer area of Ambulances (??) | Pm |
| " | 8 | | HQ's RG — arrived AILLY — Huts on lines for Pioneer Battalion selected & requisite | Pm |
| " | 9 | | Bn comm began to arrive up to strength. 11 other Ra issued — Sec. 302. 303. R F A reorganized at 4-15pm a new 4 gun & 5 Battery — 2 gun. Ammn completed & Supply tender withdrawn hours 10'd 11' | Pm |
| " | 10 | | Amm'n Park & D.S.C Amm exchange with Indian Vehicles for authorized types. The Sec. 302. 303. Brigades R.F.A arrived in the Area — 2 R.a. officers arrived to assume new units. Cavalry Ellery Staffs returned up from DOULLENS — Sub Park returning to deliver Amm to D.a.C. A&CE Report Nos 5 horsed in train Reorgainization. Ap Staff now reaching — | Pm |
| " | 11 | | 15 A.C.A. Sec these Brigades — DaC Ammn completed & Supply received — R.E. Companies & Infantry Brigades completed to strength — as limited Ammn quite rear Battalions — 20th Terns Dent — | Pm |
| " | 12 | | — Casualty changes 51 other ranks. 9 Officers & 87 other ranks. 3 — 3 Tr horses a Thigh. Div details arrived in HQ. | Tm |

Army Form C. 2118

# WAR DIARY or INTELLIGENCE SUMMARY    Co Lulu Vu

(Erase heading not required.)

Instructions regarding War Diaries and Intelligence Summaries are contained in F.S. Regs., Part II. and the Staff Manual respectively. Title Pages will be prepared in manuscript.   November 1916

| Place | Date | Hour | Summary of Events and Information | Remarks and references to Appendices |
|---|---|---|---|---|
| AILLY LE HAUT CLOCHER | 13th | | Reorganization continued. Divisional vision 1st, 2/13 Bn Lond R, 3 Cpr 2/14 Lond R. A Cpl H.W. Bulloch took over attachment of AA&QMG 60 Div vice 2 Capt F. Malcolm (to England). | Auth |
| | 14th | | Entrainment of 60 Div from LONGPRÉ to MARSEILLES begins. 1st Train departed at 7.55 a.m. Train due out at 9.15 p.m. was nearly 2 hours late. Cause of delay was -1/ Fact that 1st Train was not in to platform in time. 2/ Lack of loading facilities. [Rolls, vehicles were on No siding to entrain on 15A] hurt draft of personnel & animals. Personnel of various Brigade entrained. [Draft of 34 OR RAMC] | A/g |
| | 15th | | Entrainment continued. The entrainment generally detained by having only one yard & side to load brigades. Train due out at 11.57 a.m. did not leave until 8.25 a.m. Personnel did not get away and had not been up to prev. date. Baggage were not allowed to entrain between 6 pm and 8 am. | A/g |
| | 16th | | Entrainment continues. Delay caused to-day by two animals (mules) in each of other trains. In consequence Train due out 1.30 am and 10.45 am Bde & Inf RA Personnel did not one out in time until 1.30 pm and 4.30 pm respectively. Train due at 3.15 OR 10 am yet but had allowed to proceed until 5.30 pm on each train horses. Draft some to Base truck bridges in entrain horse. Great delay still — due to lack of loading. | A/g |
| | 17th | | Entrainment continued. Great delay. Reorganization practically complete. Train due out at 9.27 pm on 17th did not depart until 1.30 pm this day. | A/g |
| | 18th | | Entraining continues greater delay. | A/g |

Army Form C. 2118

# WAR DIARY
or
## INTELLIGENCE SUMMARY  60 DIV.
(Erase heading not required.)

NOVEMBER 1916.

Instructions regarding War Diaries and Intelligence Summaries are contained in F. S. Regs., Part II. and the Staff Manual respectively. Title Pages will be prepared in manuscript.

| Place | Date | Hour | Summary of Events and Information | Remarks and references to Appendices |
|---|---|---|---|---|
| AILLY-LE-HAUT-CLOCHER | 19th | | Entrainment continues. G.O.C. telegraphs authorising relaxation of order continuing all ranks to camp at MARSEILLES. Small percentage now allowed to leave camp. Trains leaving very late. Train 19 due out at 9.27 pm yesterday did not leave until after 1 pm today. | HM |
| | 20th | | Col Shepherd A.D.M.S. whose services were lent for reorganization of Div 60 Field Amb [Salonika] Estb has completed his work and departs for XII Corps from LONGPRÉ. Train in 2nd day link service still— | HM |
| | 21st | | Entrainment continues. Only 2 trains were sent up today - stated enroute instead of the 3 - 4½ hours late. Train 23rd was sent up wrong. Train due in at 2.27 pm to— | HM |
| | | | Entrainment continues. Train was late to training. Every endeavour made to expedite matters through loading arrival at 7.10 hrs. Local French authorities will return would A.T.O. LONGPRÉ, TRAFFIC AMIENS and LONGUEAU in own trains D.S.E. entrained at 12.0 OR for R.A, 76 OR for 2/23rd Bn. Entrainment continues. Drafts receive of 12.0 OR for R.A, 76 OR for 2/23rd Bn. | HM |
| | 22nd | | Entrainment continues. | HM |
| | 23rd | | H.Q. Div followed GOC went ADC via Paris. | HM |
| | 24th | | | |
| | 25th | | Div HQ arrive MARSEILLES and encamped CARCASSONNE | |
| | 26th | | | |
| | 27th | | | |
| | 28, 29, 30 | | MARSEILLES H.P.&.T. VERNIA to remainder to SALONIKA | |

www.ingramcontent.com/pod-product-compliance
Lightning Source LLC
Chambersburg PA
CBHW081504160426
43193CB00014B/2584